The Pressure Cooker

COOKBOOK

The Pressure Cooker

COOKBOOK

*How to Cook Quickly, Efficiently,
Healthily, and Deliciously*

Kate Rowinski

New York, New York

Good Books books may be purchased in bulk at special discounts for sales promotion, corporate gifts, fund-raising, or educational purposes. Special editions can also be created to specifications. For details, contact the Special Sales Department, Good Books, 307 West 36th Street, 11th Floor, New York, NY 10018 or info@skyhorsepublishing.com.

Good Books is an imprint of Skyhorse Publishing, Inc.®, a Delaware corporation.

Visit our website at www.goodbooks.com.

10 9 8 7 6 5 4 3 2 1

Library of Congress Cataloging-in-Publication Data is available on file.

Cover design by Owen Corrigan
Cover photo credit by Kate Rowinski

Print ISBN: 978-1-68099-063-8
Ebook ISBN: 978-1-68099-119-2

Printed in China

Table of Contents

An Introduction to Pressure Cooking

Did you think that pressure cookers belong to the era of your grandmother? Well, think again. Sure, grandma may have produced some pretty spectacular pot roasts in that rickety pot of hers. Back in her day, the pressure cooker was the ultimate convenience cookware. That's because it harnessed the power of steam to make "slaving over a hot stove" something that other people did.

How Pressure Cooking Works

When you cook with steam, the internal temperature of the pot is controlled by how much heat you apply to it. Pressure cooking follows three basic steps.

Step One:

Bring cooker to pressure. You do this by applying heat to the pot by increasing or reducing your stove's burner temperature. (If you have an electric pressure cooker, this step is accomplished by simply choosing the setting.)

Step Two:

Start counting your cooking time when the desired pressure is reached. Pressure cooking is a little different than other cooking methods in one fundamental way. The cooking time does not begin when you close the lid. Instead, you start counting when the cooker reaches its desired pressure.

Step Three:

Release pressure. This is an important step, because it dictates how fast your food will stop cooking. There are three different ways to release pressure. Use **Natural Release** when you want to allow food to continue to simmer for a little longer. Simply remove the cooker from its heat source and allow the pressure to drop on its own. It takes 15 minutes or so for the pressure to drop enough to remove the lid. Stocks and stews can be done this way. **Quick Release** of steam allows you to reduce pressure quickly so you can stop the cooking cycle. This helps to prevent overcooking, and also lets you interrupt cooking so that you can add other ingredients. **Cold Water Release** is the fastest but the least common method. Run cold water over the pot to stop the cooking process as quickly as possible. This works well for delicate foods.

The Benefits of Cooking with Pressure

Saving Time

This is the feature that generally first attracts people to pressure cooking. Pressure cooking cuts cooking time drastically; sometimes by as much as 90 percent. Any recipe that calls for a wet environment, like steaming, boiling, or stewing, is perfect for the pressure cooker. Because of the cooker's ability to maintain a hot internal environment, energy usage is drastically reduced too.

Capturing Heat

Water boils at 212 degrees Fahrenheit. But steam is actually 38 degrees hotter, about 250 degrees. By trapping the steam inside the pot, the internal cooking temperature is increased by almost 20 percent. With the steam circulating continuously around the boiling liquid, the combination of heat and pressure creates the perfect cooking environment. Especially important—because all that heat is trapped inside the pot, you can use it to make recipes that would normally overheat your kitchen, even in July.

Natural Cooking

Unlike that other modern time-saver, the microwave oven, pressure cooking is completely natural. Instead of zapping your food with harmful radiation, pressure cooking simply harnesses the steam from your cooking liquid to cook your food quickly.

Vitamin Retention

Nutrients are generally lost during the process of evaporation, but nothing escapes the pressure cooker. Well, not much anyway. Foods cooked in the pressure cooker maintain far more of their essential vitamins and minerals than foods cooked in an open environment.

Pressure Levels

Cooking with pressure is measured by how much pressure is building in the pot. This pressure measurement is called PSI, or pounds per square inch. Pressure can be controlled to three general temperatures.

High Pressure is designated as around 15 PSI. This is the temperature most used for cooking with pressure.

Medium pressure is 8–10 PSI. Steaming foods are often cooked at this temperature.

Low pressure is around 5 PSI. This temperature is used for delicate foods and vegetables.

Guidelines for Cooking with Pressure

- Never fill your pressure cooker. It needs space to perform its magic. The liquid needs room to boil, and the food needs room to expand. Food should never exceed half the pot. Liquids should never be more than about ⅔ of the pot.

- Always provide enough liquid. Water, or stock, is the engine that drives the cooking. Your pot needs enough liquid to build up its head of steam. Depending on the size of your cooker, you generally need at least a cup or two of liquid, more if you are steaming food.

- Wipe the rim of your lid before closing it. You don't want anything to get in the way of a secure seal.

- Don't guess at your processing time. Use a digital timer for more precise results.

- Never open the lid while food is cooking. The steam is extremely hot and can quickly scald skin. Fortunately, most modern pressure cookers lock in place until pressure has been safely reduced.

- Release pressure using the recommended method. Food continues to cook while under pressure, so waiting too long can ruin your recipe. Always open the lid away from you.

- In higher altitudes, liquids take longer to come to a boil, so cooking times should be increased. For every 1,000 feet above 2,000 feet, add 5 percent to your cooking time. For example, if you are at 3,000 feet in elevation, a 20 minute cooking time should be increased by one minute. At 5,000 feet, you would add 3 minutes. This may seem like a minor adjustment, but it is crucial for properly cooked recipes.

- If your food seems to have too much liquid after cooking, boil it down with the lid removed to reduce volume and consolidate flavor.

Essential Tools of the Trade

Unlike in Grandma's time, today's pressure cookers are built to be nearly foolproof, with safety features to prevent clogging and lids that lock in place to prevent peeking. There is nothing mysterious or scary about today's pressure cooker. A pressure cooker is really nothing more than a pot with a tightly fitting lid. Today's cookers are manufactured in a variety of sizes to suit almost any household, and with safety features such as triple-ply construction, locking lids, heat-resistant handles, and safe, reliable regulator valves.

The Pressure Cooker

Materials

Pressure cookers are available in aluminum and stainless steel. Aluminum versions are generally lighter and less expensive than the stainless steel versions. Aluminum conducts heat well too. They are a good choice for saving money, but not the best choice for heavy-duty use. Stainless steel cookers are heavier, with a finish that tends to stand up better to heavy use. The ideal stainless steel cooker has a layer of aluminum in the bottom of the cooker to improve heat conductivity.

Size

Pressure cookers come in a range of sizes, from two quarts to 10 quarts or more. These sizes are described in terms of total capacity of the pot, although in practice, pressure cookers are never filled to more than ½ to ⅔ of their total capacity. When choosing a size, consider what you tend to cook most often and how many people you intend to feed. Smaller cookers require less liquid and cook more quickly, but may limit your ability to handle a nice size pot of soup or one-pot meal. In addition, most cookbooks, like this one, set ingredients and cooking times to accommodate a 6-quart cooker, so if you are new at pressure cooking, you may be more comfortable following the recipes using this size pot.

If you are serious about pressure cooking, you probably will want to have at least these two sizes in your kitchen.

4-quart cooker

- Perfect for one or two people
- Handy for small batches, like side dishes and vegetables
- Cooks about 1–1½ cups of rice or grains
- Handles about 8 cups of liquid
- Great for roasts and other meats

6-quart cooker

- The most common size for households; perfect for making one-pot suppers for 4–6 people.
- A practical size for soups and chili—handles as much as 16 cups of liquid.
- Cooks up to 3 cups of grain or rice
- Most cookbook recipes are written for the 5–6 cup cooker

Electric Cooker

Electric pressure cookers take most of the guesswork out of processing time. They are designed to do the counting for you, and require no monitoring to reach pressure and cook food. This makes them a very appealing alternative to the conventional stovetop styles.

Keep in mind, though, that electric cookers can take a bit longer to reach temperature than a stovetop model. They also vary in terms of maximum pressure they can achieve, so make sure the one you buy is made for 13–15 PSI. Electric cookers generally only have two temperature settings, High and Low. Natural release of pressure takes longer too, as much as ten minutes more than a stovetop cooker.

Newer models also have browning and warming settings, a plus for executing your recipe without having to use more than one pot. Some even have a delayed start feature that lets you combine ingredients and schedule the start of cooking time.

Pressure Cooking Times for Different Ingredients

As versatile as your pressure cooker is, not all ingredients are right for it. On the other hand, it is easy to adapt many of your favorite recipes to the pressure cooker. Follow these guidelines and cooking charts for basic information on cooking with your favorite ingredients.

Meats

Pressure cooking is perfect for tougher cuts of meat, because it softens muscle fibers and naturally tenderizes them. Poultry works very well in pressure, as do pork and beef roasts. Most fish, seafood, and high quality cuts of meat are better cooked using another method, although some things do very nicely. If you do use your pressure cooker to cook fish or seafood, plan on very short processing times.

Always include a minimum of ½ cup of liquid when cooking meat. Meats cooked longer than 5 minutes require 1 cup of liquid, and larger items that will be cooked for 10 minutes or more should have 2 cups of liquid. To bring out the maximum flavor of your food, brown meat in vegetable oil before adding other ingredients. We generally use natural release pressure for beef and pork cuts, and quick release for poultry. As always, check your recipe for recommended pressure release method.

Cooking times are approximate, and may vary based on cut of meat, recipe, and pot size.

Cooking Times for Beef

WEIGHT	CUT	COOKING TIME (MIN)	PRESSURE LEVEL	RELEASE METHOD
1–2 LB	STEW MEAT, 1" CUBES	12	High	Natural
1–2 LB	BEEF MEATBALLS	8	High	Natural
2 LB	MEATLOAF	12	High	Natural
2 LB	BEEF POT ROAST	40	High	Natural
3 LB	OXTAIL	45	High	Natural
3 LB	SHORT RIBS	20	High	Natural
3 LB	ROUND OR CHUCK STEAK, 1–2" THICK	20	High	Natural

Cooking Times for Pork

WEIGHT	CUT	COOKING TIME (MIN)	PRESSURE LEVEL	RELEASE METHOD
3 LB	PORK ROAST	40	High	Natural
2 LB	PORK RIBS	15	High	Natural
2 LB	HAM SHANK	20	High	Natural
3 LB	PORK HOCKS	45	High	Natural

Cooking Times for Poultry

WEIGHT	CUT	COOKING TIME (MIN)	PRESSURE LEVEL	RELEASE METHOD
2 LB	BONELESS, SKINLESS BREAST	8	High	Quick
2–3 LB	BONE-IN BREASTS	15	High	Quick
4 LB	WHOLE CHICKEN	25	High	Quick
6 LB	BONE-IN TURKEY BREAST	30	High	Quick
3–4 LB	CHICKEN WINGS	10	High	Quick
3–5 LB	THIGHS	20	High	Quick
3 LB	WHOLE CORNISH HENS	10	High	Quick
3–4 LB	WHOLE DUCK	30	High	Quick

Cooking Times for Lamb

WEIGHT	CUT	COOKING TIME (MIN)	PRESSURE LEVEL	RELEASE METHOD
3 LB	LEG	30	High	Natural
1–2 LB	STEW MEAT, 1" CUBES	15	High	Natural

Cooking Times for Fish and Seafood

WEIGHT	CUT	COOKING TIME (MIN)	PRESSURE LEVEL	RELEASE METHOD
3 LB	WHOLE FISH	5	Low	Quick
	FISH SOUPS OR STEWS	5	High	Quick
1–2 LB	LOBSTER	3	Low	Quick
2–3 LB	MUSSELS	3	Low	Quick
3 LB	CRAB	3	Low	Quick

Vegetables

Because vegetables can be cooked so quickly in the pressure cooker, they maintain the color and flavor that is often lost with longer cooking methods. The pressure cooker is not necessarily best for delicate vegetables like asparagus, zucchini, and green beans; they require a delicate touch. But heartier vegetables like potatoes, corn, cabbage, and sturdy greens like collards and kale, are perfect for it.

To process vegetables by themselves, I prefer to use a steamer basket and place one cup of water in the pot below it. To make large batches for mashing, place vegetables and water together in pot. Use the quick release method to release pressure.

VEGETABLE	COOKING TIME (MIN)	PRESSURE LEVEL	RELEASE METHOD
ARTICHOKES, WHOLE, LARGE	10	High	Quick
GREEN BEANS	2	High	Quick
BEETS, SLICED	5	High	Quick
BEETS, WHOLE LARGE	20	High	Quick
BEETS, WHOLE SMALL	12	High	Quick
BROCCOLI STALKS	5	High	Quick
BRUSSELS SPROUTS	4	High	Quick
CABBAGE, QUARTERED	3	High	Quick
CARROTS, 1" CHUNKS	4	High	Quick
CAULIFLOWER, WHOLE	5	High	Quick
COLLARDS	5	High	Quick
CORN ON THE COB	3	High	Quick
EGGPLANT, CUT INTO CHUNKS	3	High	Quick
KALE	2	High	Quick
PARSNIPS, 1" SLICES	3	High	Quick
POTATOES FOR SALAD	7	High	Quick
POTATOES, WHOLE RED	12	High	Quick
POTATOES FOR MASHING	8	High	Quick
PUMPKIN	4	High	Quick
RUTABAGA CHUNKS	5	High	Quick
SWEET POTATOES FOR MASHING	15	High	Quick

Rice and Grains

Grains, particularly whole grains and brown rice, are a natural for the pressure cooker, Trapped steam cooks even whole grains quickly and evenly.

Rinse rice and grains before cooking. This eliminates the dusty coating of starch that can cause grains to lump together. A spoonful of oil also helps produce nice separate grains. We use the natural release method for most grains because it reduces foaming, but some grains with short processing times may be better with a quick release method.

For cooking times, we assume 1 cup of grain.

Cooking Times for Rice

	COOKING TIME (MIN)	PRESSURE LEVEL	RELEASE METHOD
SUSHI RICE	3	High	Quick
ARBORIO RICE	2	High	Quick
SHORT GRAIN WHITE RICE	4	High	Quick
LONG GRAIN WHITE RICE	5	High	Quick
SHORT GRAIN BROWN RICE	14	High	Natural
LONG GRAIN BROWN RICE	12	High	Natural
WILD RICE	20	High	Natural

Cooking Times for Grains

GRAINS	COOKING TIME (MIN)	PRESSURE LEVEL	RELEASE METHOD
KAMUT, SOAKED	13	High	Natural
OATS, STEEL CUT	11	High	Natural
WHEAT BERRIES, PRE-SOAKED	30	High	Natural

Beans

Beans and pressure cookers were made for one another! The flavor of home-cooked beans is so superior to the canned version, we can't imagine doing it any other way. And the short pressure cooker time makes bean making quick and easy.

Most beans benefit from pre-soaking to help them maintain their shape and cook more quickly. The exceptions are lentils and split peas, which do not need soaking.

Use at least 3 cups of liquid for every cup of beans. (For cooking beans by themselves, we generally use more.) Beans produce foam, which can clog the valve, so add a tablespoon of oil to the pot to alleviate the problem.

Because dried beans vary in age and moisture content, these times are approximate. For most recipes, we use the natural release method to give beans more time to finish cooking and to help them retain their shape.

Cooking Times for Beans

BEANS	PRE-SOAK?	COOKING TIME (MIN)	PRESSURE LEVEL	RELEASE METHOD
BLACK BEANS	Yes	5–6	High	Natural
BLACK-EYED PEAS	No	10	High	Natural
CANNELLINI BEANS	Yes	5	High	Natural
GARBANZOS	Yes	8	High	Natural
LENTILS, BROWN	No	8	High	Natural
NAVY BEANS	Yes	8	High	Natural
GREAT NORTHERN BEANS	Yes	5	High	Natural
PINTO BEANS	Yes	3	High	Natural
KIDNEY BEANS	Yes	5	High	Natural
SOY BEANS, BLACK	Yes	16	High	Natural
SPLIT PEAS	No	5	High	Natural

BREAKFAST

Steel Cut Oatmeal

Using a small pot or glass bowl inside your pressure cooker enables you to easily cook smaller batches and makes for easy cleanup.

1 cup steel cut oats
3 cups water
½ cup raisins
Pinch of salt
1 cup water for steaming

1. Mix the oats, 3 cups water, raisins, and salt into a bowl or pot that fits comfortably into your pressure cooker. Stir.

2. Pour one cup of water into the pressure cooker. Put the trivet in place and place the bowl on top of the trivet. Lock cooker lid and bring to high pressure. Adjust heat to maintain pressure and process on HIGH for 10 minutes. Release pressure naturally. Remove lid carefully to prevent scalding from escaping steam.

3. Serve with cream and maple syrup or brown sugar.

VARIATION

A larger batch of oats can be made directly in pressure cooker. Use a 3:1 ratio of water to oats and process for 10 minutes.

Quinoa Breakfast Porridge

Quinoa is protein rich—a great way to start the day.

3 cups water

1½ cups quinoa, rinsed and drained

1 teaspoon cinnamon

2 teaspoons vanilla extract

1. Bring water to a boil. Stir in quinoa and seasonings.

2. Lock cooker lid and bring to high pressure. Adjust heat to maintain pressure and process on HIGH for 6 minutes. Release pressure naturally. Remove lid carefully to prevent scalding from escaping steam.

3. Serve with sautéed apples, chopped pecans, and a drizzle of cream.

Eggs En Cocotte

We were first served this egg dish at a little bed-and-breakfast in Bozeman, Montana. "En cocotte" refers to the ramekin they are cooked in. Crumbled sausage and sautéed mushrooms also make a tasty base for the egg.

2 tablespoons butter
2 tablespoons diced white onion
6 ounces baby spinach
½ cup diced ham
4 large eggs
¼ cup heavy cream
1 ounce grated Swiss cheese

1. Melt butter in small skillet and add onions, cooking until just softened. Add spinach and stir until greens are well wilted. Season with salt and pepper.

2. Butter four individual ramekins. Divide diced ham into ramekins and top each with equal portions of spinach. Crack one egg into each serving and top with one tablespoon of cream over each egg. Sprinkle cheese and cover each ramekin tightly with foil.

3. Place a cup of water into the pressure cooker and insert steam rack. Place ramekins on rack. Cook at low pressure for 3–4 minutes. Quick-release the pressure. Lift steam rack carefully and remove foil from ramekins. Egg whites should be set but yolks still runny. Serve immediately.

Soft-Boiled Eggs

When it comes to eggs, I am all about the yolk. Find the freshest farm eggs you can, and serve these beauties in egg cups with buttered toast for dipping into the soft yolk.

As many eggs as you need

1. Place one cup of water in the pressure cooker. Add the steamer basket. Arrange eggs into basket. I make foil circles to stand each egg upright. That way the yolk is nicely centered for serving.

2. Close lid and process eggs on low pressure. Time 3 minutes for runny yolks, up to 5 minutes for yolks that are soft but solid. Quick release pressure, run eggs under cool water, peel, and serve.

Breakfast Casserole

A crowd-pleasing one-pot breakfast. Experiment with your own favorite vegetables.

2 tablespoons olive oil

1 small onion, diced

1 small bell pepper, diced

2 cups fresh baby spinach

½ pound crumbled pork sausage, cooked

3 cups potatoes, peeled and shredded

6 eggs, beaten

1 cup cottage cheese

2 cups mild cheddar cheese, shredded

1. Sauté onion and green pepper in hot oil until they are softened, about 5 minutes. Stir in spinach and continue to cook until wilted.

2. Add cooked sausage and potatoes. Fold in eggs, cottage cheese, and cheddar cheese.

3. Lock cooker lid and bring to high pressure. Adjust heat to maintain pressure and process on HIGH for 5 minutes. Release pressure naturally. Remove lid carefully to prevent scalding from escaping steam.

Southern-Style Grits

Old-fashioned grits beat out the instant ones every time, and with a pressure cooker, making them is a snap. Cook extra to make grit patties with the leftovers.

1 teaspoon salt
½ teaspoon black pepper
4 cups water
1 cup old-fashioned grits

1. Add salt and pepper to water. Bring to a boil. Slowly stir in grits.

2. Lock cooker lid and bring to high pressure. Adjust heat to maintain pressure and process on HIGH for 10 minutes. Release pressure naturally. Remove lid carefully to prevent scalding from escaping steam.

3. Serve hot with butter.

FOR LEFTOVER GRITS

Place leftover grits in a parchment-lined loaf pan. Place in refrigerator to chill. When ready to use, remove from pan, slice into thick slices, and fry in butter. Serve for breakfast with eggs or at dinner with your favorite sauce.

APPETIZERS AND DIPS

Deviled Eggs

Easy and consistently cooked hard-boiled eggs are a snap in the pressure cooker.

12 large eggs
½ teaspoon salt
1 teaspoon dry mustard
½ teaspoon white pepper
⅓ cup mayonnaise

1. Place one cup of water in the pressure cooker. Add the steamer basket. Arrange eggs on their sides in basket.

2. Lock cooker lid and bring to high pressure. Adjust heat to maintain pressure and process on LOW for 6 minutes. Release pressure naturally. Remove lid carefully to prevent scalding from escaping steam.

3. Remove eggs to colander. Run under cool water and peel. Cut eggs in half lengthwise. Scoop yolks into bowl, mash and mix in salt, mustard, pepper, and mayonnaise until smooth.

4. Re-fill egg whites with yolk paste, mounding up lightly. Garnish with chopped chives or a sprinkle of paprika. Serve immediately or within 24 hours.

Garlic Spread

I use this spread for everything. Eat the cloves alone, spread on toast rounds.
Or squeeze them into your favorite soup or casserole.

1 cup water
4 whole heads garlic

1. Pour water into pressure cooker. Add steamer basket. Peel away one layer of skin from each head. Cut ½ inch off top of each head to expose the individual cloves. Places whole heads into basket.

2. Lock cooker lid and bring to high pressure. Adjust heat to maintain pressure and process on HIGH for 3 minutes. Quick release pressure. Remove lid carefully to prevent scalding from escaping steam.

3. Allow the garlic to cool enough to handle. Pull out individual cloves and squeeze onto toasted French bread. Save leftover garlic to add to soups or stews.

Hummus

Sure, you can buy hummus in the store, but this one is so easy in the pressure cooker, I make a fresh batch every week. My husband likes the fact that I can control the sodium in the recipe. For him, I up the garlic and eliminate the salt.

1 cup chickpeas

6 cups water

2 cloves garlic, crushed and minced

1 tablespoon tahini

3 tablespoons lemon juice

½ teaspoon salt

White pepper

2 tablespoons olive oil

Chives or fresh parsley to garnish

1. Wash and drain chickpeas in a bowl, and then cover with water and soak overnight.

2. Drain and rinse beans again, and then place in pressure cooker with 6 cups of water. Lock cooker lid and bring to high pressure. Adjust heat to maintain pressure and process on HIGH for 15 minutes. Release pressure naturally. Remove lid carefully to prevent scalding from escaping steam.

3. Drain beans, reserving 1 cup of cooking liquid for thinning paste. Allow beans to cool. Puree cooled beans using an immersion blender.

4. Add minced garlic, tahini, and lemon juice, and continue to blend, adding a little of the cooking liquid as you go, until you reach the desired consistency. Season with salt and a couple of grinds of white pepper.

5. Place hummus in serving bowl and add a drizzle of olive oil over the top. Garnish with chopped parsley or chives.

Mini Meatballs

I love my meatballs long-simmered and tender. The pressure cooker achieves this result in just 10 minutes.
Use barbecue sauce or your own favorite red sauce.

½ pound ground pork
½ pound ground beef
1 large egg
½ cup seasoned bread crumbs
2 tablespoons milk
¼ cup diced onion
1 garlic clove, minced
½ teaspoon salt
¼ teaspoon pepper

2 cups barbecue sauce

1. Mix all meatball ingredients in a bowl, adjusting milk and breadcrumbs to get a firm consistency.

2. Form 2 dozen small meatballs and place in pressure cooker. Lock cooker lid and bring to high pressure. Adjust heat to maintain pressure and process on HIGH for 10 minutes. Quick release pressure. Remove lid carefully to prevent scalding from escaping steam.

3. Remove meatballs from pressure cooker and drain cooking liquid. Place two cups of barbecue sauce (or your own favorite sauce) in pot and bring to a simmer. Add meatballs back into sauce and stir to coat. Allow to simmer together for 10 minutes.

4. Serve warm with crusty bread.

Classic Steamed Mussels

Practically instant mussels. I make these as a first course in the pressure cooker while the rest of the meal simmers on the stove.

2 pounds fresh mussels

1 tablespoon olive oil

2 shallots, minced

1 clove garlic, minced

½ cup white wine

½ cup water

1. Clean mussels and remove beards. Discard any that are not tightly closed. Arrange evenly in steamer basket, and set aside.

2. Heat the pressure cooker and add olive oil. Sauté shallots and garlic until softened. Add white wine and water, and then place the steamer basket in place. Adjust heat to maintain pressure and process on LOW for 1 minute. Quick release pressure. Remove lid carefully to prevent scalding from escaping steam.

3. Remove steamer basket and transfer mussels to a large bowl. Pour steaming liquid over mussels and serve with crusty bread.

Apricot Barbecue Chicken Wings

Tender, juicy wings…adapt to your own sauce to make the recipe your own!

2 tablespoons vegetable oil
24 chicken wings
½ cup apricot preserves
½ cup prepared barbecue sauce
I package dry onion soup mix
I cup water
Sesame seeds, as desired

1. Place oil in pressure cooker and heat. Add chicken wings, turning until browned on all sides.

2. Combine apricot, sauce, water, and onion soup mix. Pour over wings and stir to coat evenly.

3. Lock cooker lid and bring to high pressure. Adjust heat to maintain pressure and process on HIGH for 10 minutes. Quick release pressure. Remove lid carefully to prevent scalding from escaping steam.

4. Remove wings to serving platter and continue to cook sauce to reduce to desired consistency. Brush thickened sauce over wings and serve. Coat with sesame seeds if preferred.

Eggplant-amole

A variation on the classic baba ghanoush—this one has a little extra kick of chili powder.

4 pounds eggplant

2 cups water

1 teaspoon salt

1 tablespoon + 1 tablespoon olive oil

½ small onion, chopped

3 cloves garlic, peeled and minced

1 tomato, diced

3 tablespoons fresh parsley

1 tablespoon red wine vinegar

½ teaspoon chili powder

Salt and pepper

1. Peel eggplants and cut into large cubes. Place chunks in bowl and toss with salt. Set aside for 10 minutes.

2. Place eggplant and water in pressure cooker. Lock cooker lid and bring to high pressure. Adjust heat to maintain pressure and process on HIGH for 5 minutes. Naturally release pressure. Remove lid carefully to prevent scalding from escaping steam. Remove eggplant from cooking liquid and allow to cool.

3. While eggplant is cooling, heat 1 tablespoon olive oil and sauté onion until slightly caramelized. Add garlic and cook another 60 seconds to release fragrance. Remove from heat and set aside.

4. Pulse eggplant in food processor to desired consistency. Transfer to a large bowl and add onion, garlic, tomato, parsley, 1 tablespoon olive oil, vinegar, and chili powder; stir to combine. Adjust seasonings to taste.

5. Serve with crisp pita chips.

SOUPS AND CHILI

Beef Stock

So much better than store-bought, this recipe allows you to use all your leftovers and make them into a tasty base. I freeze batches in plastic containers so there is always some on hand.

2 tablespoon olive oil

4 pounds meaty bones from the butcher

½ pound stew meat or trimming scraps

2 onions, peeled and quartered

2 carrots, peeled and cut into chunks

¼ cup tomato paste

Celery tops or a couple of ribs

2–3 cloves garlic

Fresh parsley

2 bay leaves

8–10 peppercorns

8 cups water

1. Place oil in pressure cooker and brown bones and scraps on all sides. Remove beef to a bowl as pieces are browned.

2. Add onions and carrots to pot and sauté for 5 minutes, until softened. Stir in tomato paste. Return beef to pot and add celery, garlic, parsley, bay leaves, and peppercorns. Pour in water and stir.

3. Lock cooker lid and bring to high pressure. Adjust heat to maintain pressure and process on HIGH for 1 hour. Release pressure naturally. Remove lid carefully to prevent scalding from escaping steam.

4. Spoon excess fat from the top of the pot, remove the bones and vegetables, and strain stock into another pot through a fine mesh sieve. Let cool to room temperature and then refrigerate.

5. When ready to use, remove any solid fat from the top of the stock and discard. Freeze extra stock for later use.

Chicken Stock

Ever wonder what to do with that leftover chicken carcass? Here's the answer.

Leftover bones and skin from a roasted chicken

2 onions, peeled and quartered

2 carrots, peeled and cut into chunks

Celery tops or a couple of celery ribs

Fresh parsley

2 bay leaves

8–10 peppercorns

8 cups water

1. Place the chicken carcass and all the rest of the ingredients into the pressure cooker and cover with water.

2. Lock cooker lid and bring to high pressure. Adjust heat to maintain pressure and process on HIGH for 50 minutes. Release pressure naturally. Remove lid carefully to prevent scalding from escaping steam.

3. Spoon excess fat from the top of the pot, remove the bones and vegetables, and strain stock into another pot through a fine mesh sieve. Let cool to room temperature and then refrigerate.

4. When ready to use, remove any solid fat from the top of the stock and discard. Freeze extra stock for later use.

Vegetable Stock

The beauty of this vegetable stock is that you can take it any direction you prefer. Experiment with your favorite vegetables, add more tomatoes, or leave them out all together!

1 large onion, quartered

2–3 carrots, cut into chunks

Celery tops or a couple of celery ribs

3 cloves garlic

1 leek, green and white, chopped

1 parsnip

1 tomato, chopped

4–5 sprigs fresh thyme

1 bay leaf

1 bunch parsley

10 peppercorns

8 cups water

1. Place all the ingredients into pressure cooker and cover with water.

2. Lock cooker lid and bring to high pressure. Adjust heat to maintain pressure and process on HIGH for 30 minutes. Release pressure naturally. Remove lid carefully to prevent scalding from escaping steam.

3. Remove the vegetables, and strain stock into another pot through a fine mesh sieve. Let cool to room temperature and then refrigerate. Freeze extra stock for later use.

Ham Stock

A southern staple—and a great base for bean and pork dishes.

2 ham hocks

Water

1. Place ham hocks in pressure cooker and add water up to the fill line.

2. Lock cooker lid and bring to high pressure. Adjust heat to maintain pressure and process on MEDIUM for 45 minutes. Release pressure naturally. Remove lid carefully to prevent scalding from escaping steam.

3. Remove hocks and set aside. Spoon excess fat from the top of the pot and strain stock into another pot through a fine mesh sieve. Let cool to room temperature and then refrigerate.

4. When ready to use, remove any solid fat from the top of the stock and discard. Freeze extra stock for later use.

Carrot and Apple Soup with Ginger

Light, bright flavors and glorious color. Serve as a festive first course with a swirl of sour cream.

½ stick butter
2 tablespoons fresh ginger, grated
4 tablespoons soy sauce
4 apples, sliced
4 cups carrots, peeled and sliced
2 tablespoons lemon juice
6 cups vegetable stock
1 cup yogurt
Salt and pepper

1. Melt butter in pot. Add ginger and soy sauce, and sauté until smooth and bubbly. Add apples, carrots, and lemon juice, stirring to coat all ingredients. Stir in stock.

2. Lock cooker lid and bring to high pressure. Adjust heat to maintain pressure and process on HIGH for 7 minutes. Quick release pressure. Remove lid carefully to prevent scalding from escaping steam.

3. Puree soup using an immersion blender until very smooth. Stir in yogurt, adjust seasonings, and serve.

Navy Bean and Kielbasa Soup

Rich and meaty, this soup is the perfect winter time or après-ski meal.

1 pound dried navy beans, rinsed

2 tablespoons oil

1 large onion, chopped

4 ribs celery, chopped

4 carrots, chopped

1 clove garlic, minced

1 pound kielbasa, sliced

10 cups chicken stock

1 teaspoon dried thyme

2 teaspoons salt

1/4 teaspoon freshly ground pepper

1. Soak beans overnight. Drain and rinse thoroughly. Set aside.

2. Place oil in pressure cooker. Sauté onions, celery, and carrots until onions are translucent. Add garlic and kielbasa and stir to coat.

3. Stir in drained beans, chicken stock, and seasonings. Lock cooker lid and bring to high pressure. Adjust heat to maintain pressure and process on HIGH for 30 minutes. Let pressure release naturally. Remove lid carefully to prevent scalding from escaping steam.

4. Use an immersion blender to puree beans, if desired.

Chicken Noodle Soup

About once a month, my family demands this soup. So much better than anything you can buy ready-made, it is well worth the time. I often make the base soup, and then let family members add the noodles or rice of their choice.

3–4 bone-in chicken breasts (about 3 lbs)
1 onion, finely chopped
2 carrots, peeled and sliced
2 celery ribs, sliced ½-inch thick
2 cloves garlic, minced
6 cups hot water
½ teaspoon thyme
1 bay leaf
1 tablespoon salt
1 teaspoon sugar
¼ teaspoon black pepper
1 cup egg noodles
Parsley
Fresh lemon wedges

1. Place chicken, breast sides up, in the bottom of the pressure cooker. Add onion, carrots, celery, and garlic. Pour in water, and add thyme, bay leaf, salt, sugar, and black pepper.

2. Lock cooker lid and bring to high pressure. Adjust heat to maintain pressure and process on HIGH for 20 minutes. Quick release pressure. Remove lid carefully to prevent scalding from escaping steam.

3. Remove chicken and allow pieces to cool. Remove meat from bones and cut into bite-size pieces.

4. Skim fat from the surface of the broth. Before serving, bring broth to a boil and add noodles. Cook until tender. Add shredded chicken back to pot to re-warm. Adjust seasonings; garnish with fresh parsley and a squeeze of fresh lemon.

Classic Home-style Chili

Twenty-minute chili that tastes like it took all day.

3 pounds lean ground beef

1 tablespoon vegetable oil

1 large onion, diced

1 medium green pepper, diced

2 cloves garlic

4 cups tomato puree

2 cups beef stock

¼ cup chili powder

2 teaspoons cumin

1 teaspoon Mexican oregano

1 teaspoon salt

2 15-oz cans kidney beans, drained and rinsed

1. Sauté ground beef in oil until evenly browned. Drain excess oil and place back on heat. Add onion, pepper, and garlic, cooking until softened, about 5 minutes.

2. Add tomato puree, beef stock, chili powder, cumin, oregano, and salt.

3. Lock cooker lid and bring to high pressure. Adjust heat to maintain pressure and process on LOW for 15 minutes. Let pressure release naturally. Remove lid carefully to prevent scalding from escaping steam.

4. Stir in beans, cooking until heated through.

5. Serve topped with shredded cheddar cheese and chopped onions, and with tortilla chips, crusty bread, or soda crackers on the side.

Chilled Borscht

Cold soups are a summertime treat, especially when you don't have to
overheat a hot kitchen to get it ready to serve.

I large onion, chopped

2 tablespoons butter

I pound beets, peeled and cut
into ¼-inch matchsticks

I pound potatoes, peeled and
cut into ¾-inch cubes

3 large carrots, peeled and
sliced

½ head cabbage, shredded

6 cups beef stock

2 bay leaves

Salt and pepper to taste

3 tablespoons lemon juice

Sour cream to garnish

1. Sauté onion in butter until translucent. Add beets, potatoes, carrots, and cabbage, along with beef stock and bay leaves.

2. Lock cooker lid and bring to high pressure. Adjust heat to maintain pressure and process on HIGH for 10 minutes. Quick release pressure. Remove lid carefully to prevent scalding from escaping steam.

3. Remove bay leaves, adjust seasonings, and stir in lemon juice. Place in large bowl, cover, and chill.

4. Serve with dollops of sour cream.

Lentils and Vegetable Soup

A hearty pot of lentils with a hefty portion of vegetables. Make it purely vegetarian by using vegetable broth instead of chicken broth.

1 large white onion, chopped

2 ribs celery, chopped

2 large carrots, peeled and chopped

2 tablespoons olive oil

2 cloves garlic, minced

2 cups dried lentils

1½ quarts chicken stock

2 tablespoons tomato paste

1 teaspoon salt

½ teaspoon black pepper

1 teaspoon dried thyme

2 bay leaves

1 potato, peeled and chopped

2 tablespoons red wine vinegar

1. Sauté onion, celery, and carrots in oil until softened. Add garlic and continue to cook for another 60 seconds.

2. Add the lentils, chicken stock, and tomato paste, stirring to combine. Stir in salt, pepper, and thyme, and add bay leaves and potato to the pot.

3. Lock cooker lid and bring to high pressure. Adjust heat to maintain pressure and process on HIGH for 10 minutes. Naturally release pressure. Remove lid carefully to prevent scalding from escaping steam.

4. Stir in red wine vinegar to finish. Serve warm with crusty bread.

Cauliflower Leek Soup

My paleo-loving daughter asked me to make her a comforting white soup.
This is the result, made extra special with a garnish of bacon.

1 medium onion, chopped

4 large leeks, green and white, thinly sliced

3 tablespoons vegetable oil

1 large head cauliflower, chopped

¾ cup chopped celery

3 cups chicken stock

1 teaspoon dried thyme

2 tablespoons butter

2 tablespoons flour

½ cup heavy cream

½ teaspoon salt

¼ teaspoon black pepper

⅛ teaspoon nutmeg

Crumbled bacon and shredded cheese to garnish

1. Sauté onions and leeks in vegetable oil until soft. Add cauliflower, celery, chicken stock, and thyme into pressure cooker.

2. Lock cooker lid and bring to high pressure. Adjust heat to maintain pressure and process on HIGH for 10 minutes. Quick release pressure. Remove lid carefully to prevent scalding from escaping steam.

3. While cauliflower is cooking, make a blond roux of butter and flour by melting butter in small saucepan. Add flour and stir constantly over low heat until roux thickens and browns to a light tan. Set aside. Use stick blender to mash cauliflower to desired consistency.

4. Whisk roux into soup and simmer for a few minutes to thicken. Stir in cream and season with salt, pepper, and nutmeg.

5. Serve with crumbled bacon and shredded cheese.

French Onion Soup

French onion soup can be really time-consuming, but this version is a snap.
I would never make my onion base any other way!

6 cups yellow onions, thinly sliced

2 tablespoons + 6 tablespoons butter

2 tablespoons oil

1 teaspoon salt

1 teaspoon sugar

½ cup white wine or dry vermouth

1 teaspoon Worcestershire sauce

6 cups beef stock

4 tablespoons flour

3 tablespoons Cognac (optional)

French bread cubes

Gruyère or Monterey Jack cheese, shredded

1. Sauté onions in 2 tablespoons butter and oil, stirring frequently. Season with salt and sugar, cooking until nicely browned, about 20 minutes. Add white wine, stirring to deglaze the pan. Simmer gently for a couple of minutes to burn off alcohol. Add Worcestershire sauce and beef stock.

2. Lock cooker lid and bring to high pressure. Adjust heat to maintain pressure and process on HIGH for 6 minutes. Quick release pressure. Remove lid carefully to prevent scalding from escaping steam.

3. While onions are cooking, make a blond roux of butter and flour by melting 4 tablespoons of butter in small saucepan. Add flour and stir constantly over low heat until roux thickens and browns to a light tan. Set aside.

4. Remove 1 cup onion broth and whisk into the roux to temper it. When broth is incorporated into roux, stir it into the pot and simmer for a few minutes to thicken. Finish with Cognac.

5. When you are ready to serve, turn oven broiler to high. Divide onion soup into individual oven proof crocks. Place cubes of French bread into each bowl and top with shredded cheese. Place crocks under hot broiler until cheese is browned and bubbly. Remove from oven and serve immediately.

Garden Fresh Tomato Soup

I am not a fan of conventional tomato soup, but this version is in a class of its own.
Try it with fresh farmer's market tomatoes.

6 cups fresh tomatoes, washed

2 medium onions, diced

3 stalks celery, diced

2 carrots, peeled and grated

2 tablespoons olive oil

1½ quarts homemade vegetable stock

1 tablespoon fresh oregano, minced

12 fresh basil leaves, minced

1 teaspoon salt

½ teaspoon black pepper

Sour cream for garnish

1. Grate tomatoes into a large bowl to capture the juice and pulp (for a smoother soup, peel and seed them first, and then chop the pulp, making sure to capture as much juice as you can).

2. Sauté the onions, celery, and carrots in the oil, cooking until they have softened. Add the tomatoes and vegetable stock. Lock cooker lid and bring to high pressure. Adjust heat to maintain pressure and process on HIGH for 5 minutes. Naturally release pressure. Remove lid carefully to prevent scalding from escaping steam.

3. Stir in fresh herbs and add salt and pepper. Use an immersion blender to puree all ingredients. For a creamy soup, swirl a spoonful of sour cream into each bowl.

Vegetable Beef Soup

*Classic comfort food in a snap—no need to get out the slow cooker in the morning
when this can be on the table in less than a half hour.*

2 tablespoons vegetable oil

1 pound beef stew meat, cut
into ½-inch cubes

1 cup chopped onions

2 cloves garlic, minced

6 cups beef stock

1 15-oz can diced tomatoes

2 tablespoons tomato paste

1 teaspoon salt

1 teaspoon dried thyme

2 bay leaves

5 black peppercorns

1 cup celery chopped into
½-inch slices

1 cup carrots chopped into
½-inch slices

1 pound potatoes, cut into
¾-inch cubes

2 cups frozen corn, peas, or
greens beans

1. Heat oil in pot and sauté beef until browned on all sides. Add onions and garlic, and continue to cook until onions are translucent. Add stock, tomatoes, and paste along with seasonings, celery, carrots, and potatoes.

2. Lock cooker lid and bring to high pressure. Adjust heat to maintain pressure and process on HIGH for 15 minutes. Quick release pressure. Remove lid carefully to prevent scalding from escaping steam.

3. Stir in frozen corn, peas, or green beans and heat until warmed through. Taste and adjust seasonings as needed.

4. Serve with crusty bread.

Vichyssoise

I love this soup, extra rich and extra creamy, with the subtle flavor of chives.

1 large onion, sliced

3 tablespoons butter

2 pounds potatoes, cut into
¾-inch cubes

½ cup chopped celery

4 cups chicken stock

½ teaspoon salt

½ cup sour cream

½ cup heavy cream

Salt and pepper to taste

Fresh chopped chives

1. Sauté onion in butter, cooking until translucent. Stir in potatoes, celery, chicken stock, and salt.

2. Lock cooker lid and bring to high pressure. Adjust heat to maintain pressure and process on HIGH for 10 minutes. Quick release pressure. Remove lid carefully to prevent scalding from escaping steam.

3. Pour contents of cooker into a large bowl. Use stick blender to puree potatoes until very smooth. Stir in sour cream and heavy cream, and season with salt and pepper to taste. Cover and chill.

4. When ready to serve, taste and adjust seasonings. Garnish with chopped chives.

White Chili

Authentic New Mexico flavor in a fraction of the time.

I pound navy or great northern beans, soaked overnight, drained and rinsed

6 cups chicken stock

8 fresh roasted and peeled Anaheim or poblano chiles

I medium onion, chopped

2 cloves garlic, blanched and minced

2–3 jalapeños, chopped

I tablespoon vegetable oil

¼ cup Pendery's White Chile Blend

4 cups diced cooked chicken

Salt to taste

Sour cream

Fresh chopped cilantro

1. Combine pre-soaked beans and chicken stock in pressure cooker. Lock cooker lid and bring to high pressure. Adjust heat to maintain pressure and process on HIGH for 15 minutes. Quick release pressure. Remove lid carefully to prevent scalding from escaping steam.

2. Roast fresh whole green chiles by placing them on a hot grill, turning with tongs until they are charred on all sides. When they are cool, rub the blackened peel off and rinse. Remove stems, cut in half lengthwise, remove seeds, and dice. Set aside.

3. In a separate skillet, sauté onion, garlic, and jalapeños in oil until tender. Add in green chiles and all seasonings, stirring to incorporate. Transfer seasoned mix into the bean mixture with chicken.

4. Lock cooker lid back into place and bring to high pressure. Adjust heat to maintain pressure and process on HIGH for 5 minutes. Quick release pressure. Remove lid carefully to prevent scalding from escaping steam.

5. Taste and salt before serving. Serve topped with sour cream and a garnish of chopped cilantro.

BEEF AND PORK

Asian Barbecue Short Ribs

Tender and delicious, with a ginger and garlic glaze.

2 tablespoons olive oil

3 pounds boneless beef short ribs

¼ cup green onions, green and white, chopped

½ cup soy sauce

½ cup beef broth

1 tablespoon brown sugar

1 tablespoon fresh ginger, minced

2 cloves garlic, minced

½ teaspoon black pepper

1 tablespoon sesame seeds

1. Heat oil in cooker. Sauté short ribs until browned on all sides, 3–4 minutes on each side.

2. Combine onions, soy sauce, broth, brown sugar, ginger, garlic, and pepper in a small bowl. Pour over ribs.

3. Lock cooker lid and bring to high pressure. Adjust heat to maintain pressure and process on HIGH for 60 minutes. Let pressure release naturally. Remove lid carefully to prevent scalding from escaping steam.

4. Remove meat from liquid with tongs and set aside. Let liquid cool slightly and skim excess fat. Bring liquid back to a boil, cooking to reduce by half. Lower heat and stir in sesame oil. Return meat to pot and simmer for 15 minutes.

5. Serve over rice if preferred, garnishing meat with sesame seeds.

Beef Stroganoff

This recipe used to take me hours. I get the same result—tender, succulent beef and mushrooms—in just 20 minutes.

3 tablespoons vegetable oil

2 pounds beef stew meat,
1-inch cubes

1 teaspoon salt

½ teaspoon black pepper

2 tablespoons flour

1 medium onion, chopped

2 cloves garlic, minced

1 cup beef stock

8 ounces fresh mushrooms,
sliced

2 tablespoons tomato paste

1 tablespoon Worcestershire
sauce

½ cup sour cream

4 cups hot cooked egg noodles

1 tablespoon butter

1 teaspoon poppy seeds

1. Place oil in pressure cooker and bring it to high heat. Season beef with salt and pepper, and then place meat in oil and brown until very brown on all sides.

2. Sprinkle beef cubes with flour, and add in onion, garlic, beef stock, mushrooms, tomato paste, and Worcestershire sauce.

3. Lock cooker lid and bring to high pressure. Adjust heat to maintain pressure and process on HIGH for 20 minutes. Quick release pressure. Remove lid carefully to prevent scalding from escaping steam.

4. Allow to simmer with lid off to bring sauce to desired consistency. Stir in sour cream. Prepare egg noodles, and toss with butter and poppy seeds.

5. Serve beef over hot buttered egg noodles.

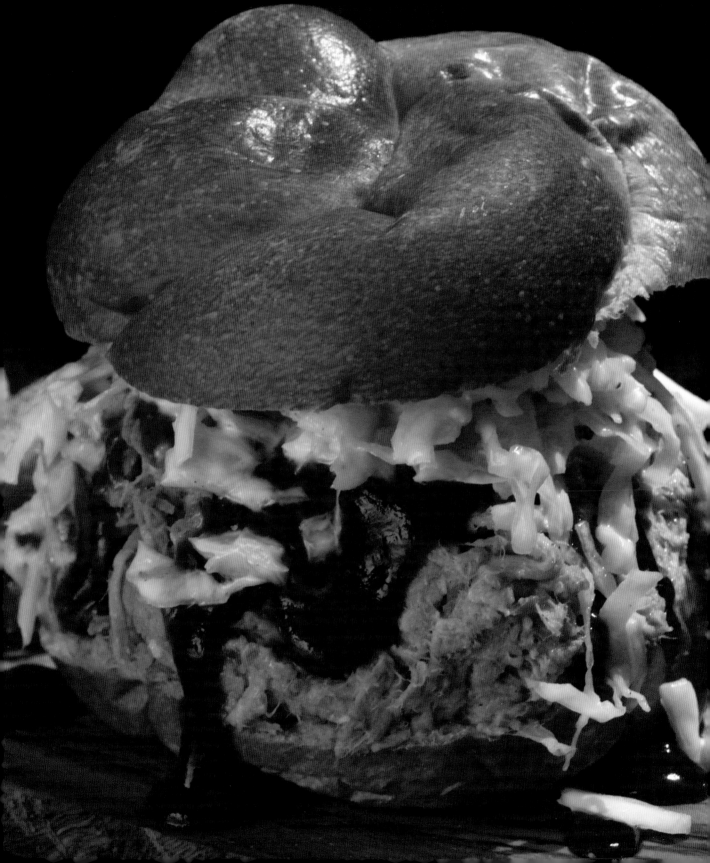

Beer-B-Que Pork

This is our grandson's favorite barbecue dish. His daddy, Luther, came up with this simple recipe. Keeping it simple is the best way to bring out the combined flavors of pork tenderloin and a great beer. Experiment with your favorite beers to make this your own recipe.

2 tablespoons vegetable oil

1 3-pound pork tenderloin, cut in half

1 medium onion, sliced into thin rings

12-ounce bottle beer

1. Place oil in pressure cooker and turn to medium heat. Add pork and brown on all sides.

2. Nestle two pieces together and place onion slices on top. Pour beer over the top.

3. Lock cooker lid and bring to high pressure. Adjust heat to maintain pressure and process on HIGH for 45 minutes. Quick release pressure. Remove lid carefully to prevent scalding from escaping steam.

4. Shred pork with a fork. Serve on sandwich rolls with a squeeze of barbecue sauce and vinegar-based cole slaw.

St. Patrick's Day Corned Beef Dinner

We have a hard time making enough of this at our restaurant on St. Patty's Day.
A simple, classic Irish dish.

2 medium onions, sliced

4 pounds corned beef with spice packet

2 cups broth

12-ounce bottle beer

2 cloves garlic, peeled

1 pound small red potatoes

12 baby carrots

1 head green cabbage, quartered

1. Place onions in bottom of pressure cooker pot. Set corned beef on top of onions, and add broth, beer, spice packet, and garlic. Bring to a boil and cook for 5 minutes to burn off alcohol.

2. Lock cooker lid and bring to high pressure. Adjust heat to maintain pressure and process on HIGH for 1 hour 20 minutes. Quick release pressure. Remove lid carefully to prevent scalding from escaping steam.

3. Remove meat and onions to a serving dish. Add potatoes, carrots, and cabbage to liquid. Close cooker and process on HIGH for 6 minutes. Quick release pressure.

4. Serve vegetables with corned beef and onions, using cooking liquid as needed to moisten the meat.

Flemish Beef Stew

A mellow brown Belgian ale is our favorite beer to use in this dish; most stouts are too strong.
This is a nice change of pace to a standard beef stew, with the brown ale adding richness to its flavor.

10 ounces bacon, cut into ½-inch pieces

2 pounds beef chuck roast, cut into 2-inch cubes

2 tablespoons flour

½ teaspoon salt

½ teaspoon black pepper

2 tablespoons extra virgin olive oil

1 medium yellow onion, chopped

1 large carrot, chopped

2 stalks celery, chopped

4 cloves garlic, minced

12-ounce bottle dark beer

2 cups beef stock

1 tablespoon whole-grain mustard

10 prunes, whole

1 green apple, medium dice

1. Heat pressure cooker over medium heat. Add bacon and cook until crisp. Transfer bacon to a bowl, and pour out most of the fat, leaving two tablespoons in pot.

2. Toss beef cubes in flour, salt, and pepper. Add to the pot and brown in bacon fat on all sides. Remove beef chunks and set aside.

3. Reduce heat and add olive oil. Sauté onion, carrot, celery, and garlic until softened. Return the bacon and beef to the pot. Add the beer, beef stock, and mustard, and top with prunes and apple.

4. Lock cooker lid and bring to high pressure. Adjust heat to maintain pressure and process on HIGH for 25 minutes. Quick release pressure. Remove lid carefully to prevent scalding from escaping steam.

5. Serve over roasted potatoes.

Hometown Meatloaf

We love meatloaf, especially in the fall and winter months. Whenever you crave comfort food, prepare this easy recipe.

1 cup dry bread crumbs

1 cup milk

1½ pounds ground beef

1 egg

1 small onion, minced

1 clove garlic, minced

1 teaspoon Worcestershire sauce

1½ teaspoons salt

½ teaspoon dried mustard

¼ teaspoon black pepper

¼ teaspoon ground sage

½ cup prepared barbecue sauce, ketchup, or brown gravy

1. Combine bread crumbs and milk. Mix in ground beef and egg, along with onion, garlic, Worcestershire sauce, and seasonings.

2. Form meat into two firm loaves. Place them side by side in the center of a sheet of aluminum foil and lower into pressure cooker.

3. Lock cooker lid and bring to high pressure. Adjust heat to maintain pressure and process on HIGH for 15 minutes. Quick release pressure. Remove lid carefully to prevent scalding from escaping steam.

4. Spread ½ cup sauce over meatloaves and let them rest in open pressure cooker for 10 minutes. Lift out of cooker, transfer to platter, and serve.

Italian Oxtails

Slow-simmered flavors with all the natural juices preserved,
but in a quarter of the time.

1 tablespoon red wine vinegar

3 tablespoons + 2 tablespoons olive oil

2 tablespoons fennel seeds

4 pounds beef oxtail, cut into 2-inch lengths

2 medium onions, quartered

2 bay leaves

2½ cups red wine

1. Whisk vinegar and 3 tablespoons oil together. Crush fennel seeds and add to the oil. Place oxtails in a one-gallon resealable bag and pour the marinade over them, turning to coat each piece. Refrigerate overnight, turning bag occasionally to coat meat evenly.

2. Place 2 tablespoons olive oil in cooker. Remove oxtails from marinade and cook until browned on all sides, 3–4 minutes on each side. Set oxtails aside after browning.

3. Place onions and bay leaves in the bottom of the pot, and then place the oxtails on top. Pour wine over meat, increase heat, and bring to a boil. Boil for a few minutes to burn off alcohol.

4. Lock cooker lid and bring to high pressure. Adjust heat to maintain pressure and process on HIGH for 60 minutes. Let pressure release naturally. Remove lid carefully to prevent scalding from escaping steam.

5. Serve oxtails with buttered egg noodles, if preferred. Garnish with chopped parsley.

Perfect Pot Roast

The aroma of a pot roast simmering on the top of the stove all Sunday afternoon is great,
but who has the time? No need to wait all day for your favorite meal!

3-pound beef sirloin tip roast

Salt and pepper

¼ cup all-purpose flour

1 tablespoon vegetable oil

1 large yellow onion, sliced

3 carrots, sliced

1 cup beef stock

½ cup red wine

2 garlic cloves, minced

½ teaspoon dried thyme

1 bay leaf

4 potatoes, peeled and cut into large chunks

4 large carrots, cut into large chunks

1. Pat the roast dry with paper towels. Rub salt and pepper onto both sides and roll in flour to coat.

2. Place oil in pressure cooker and heat briefly before adding the roast. Brown beef on all sides and then remove it and set aside. Add onion and sauté until slices start to turn tender. Place the roast on top of onions and add carrots, stock, wine, garlic, thyme, and bay leaf.

3. Lock cooker lid and bring to high pressure. Adjust heat to maintain pressure and process on HIGH for 30 minutes. Quick release pressure. Remove lid carefully to prevent scalding from escaping steam.

4. Add potatoes and additional carrots to the pot. Lock cooker lid again and bring back to high pressure. Adjust heat to maintain pressure and process on HIGH for 15 minutes. Quick release pressure. Remove lid carefully to prevent scalding from escaping steam.

5. Transfer roast and whole vegetables to serving plate. Cover with foil and allow it to rest for 5 minutes. To thicken sauce, blend carrots and onions into the juices. Adjust seasonings, pour over meat, and serve.

Pork Roast with Onions and Sauerkraut

A German twist on your traditional pot roast.

3-pound pork boneless top loin roast

4 cloves garlic, minced

1 teaspoon salt

½ teaspoon pepper

3 tablespoons vegetable oil

2 large onions, sliced

1 Granny Smith apple, coarsely chopped

1 ½ cups chicken stock

1 lb sauerkraut, rinsed and drained

1. Rub pork with garlic, salt, and pepper. Heat oil in pressure cooker and add pork roast, cooking until browned on all sides.

2. Add onions, apple, and chicken stock and cook until onions are softened. Add sauerkraut.

3. Lock cooker lid and bring to high pressure. Adjust heat to maintain pressure and process on HIGH for 40 minutes. Quick release pressure. Remove lid carefully to prevent scalding from escaping steam.

Sausage and Sauerkraut

In Wisconsin, German sausage was a staple in our weekly menu.
Here is a great one-pot version of the dish.

1 pound fresh sauerkraut

1 cup white wine

1 cup chicken stock

1 pound red potatoes, halved

½ pound salt pork, sliced

2 pound assorted sausages, knockwurst, bratwurst, or other German style sausage

1. Drain and rinse sauerkraut. Place sauerkraut into a pressure cooker; pour in white wine and chicken stock. Add potatoes and salt pork cubes.

2. Lock cooker lid and bring to high pressure. Adjust heat to maintain pressure and process on HIGH for 10 minutes. Quick release pressure. Remove lid carefully to prevent scalding from escaping steam.

3. Add sausages and lock cooker lid back into place. Return to high pressure. Adjust heat to maintain pressure and process on HIGH for 5 minutes. Quick release pressure. Remove lid carefully to prevent scalding from escaping steam.

4. Garnish with cooked apples and carrots.

Rosemary Pork Tenderloin

Simple and fragrant, with a lovely flavor of garlic and tangy mustard.

3 tablespoons oil

4-pound pork tenderloin

3 tablespoons olive oil

3 tablespoons chopped rosemary leaves

3 tablespoons coarse mustard

6 cloves garlic, minced

Salt and pepper

1 cup chicken stock

1. Place oil in pressure cooker and turn to medium heat. Cut loin in half. Brown each loin on all sides.

2. Combine olive oil, rosemary leaves, mustard, garlic, ½ teaspoon salt and black pepper. Rub over top of pork loin pieces. Nestle both pieces together in pot. Pour in chicken stock.

3. Lock cooker lid and bring to high pressure. Adjust heat to maintain pressure and process on HIGH for 25 minutes. Quick release pressure. Remove lid carefully to prevent scalding from escaping steam.

4. Remove loin from oven and let rest before slicing. Continue to simmer pan sauce until desired consistency.

Shredded Beef Sandwiches

Tender and juicy with a hint of spicy from the peperoncini.
These are a favorite at autumn tailgates.

1–4 pound rump roast, cut into
2-inch chunks

Salt and pepper

2 tablespoons vegetable oil

1 large onion, sliced thin

1 16-ounce jar peperoncini,
with juice

2 cups beef stock

1. Toss beef chunks with salt and pepper. Heat oil in pressure cooker. Add beef and brown on all sides. Place sliced onion on top of beef. Add peperoncini. Pour in beef stock.

2. Lock cooker lid and bring to high pressure. Adjust heat to maintain pressure and process on HIGH for 30 minutes. Quick release pressure. Remove lid carefully to prevent scalding from escaping steam.

3. Remove beef to large bowl. Use two forks to shred meat, peppers, and onion together. Pour enough juice over meat to moisten. Pile beef onto crusty rolls and serve.

Swiss Steak

A great way to turn a not-so-tender slice of steak into a mouthwatering meal in no time. A sure-fire recipe with hungry boys.

3 slices bacon

Salt and pepper

1½–2 pounds round steak, cut into large cubes

1 14.5-ounce can diced tomatoes

½ cup red wine

1½ cups beef broth

¼ teaspoon cayenne

½ cup chopped onions

¼ cup chopped green bell pepper

2 stalks celery, chopped

1. Cook bacon slices in pressure cooker until crispy. Remove bacon and set aside.

2. Salt and pepper beef cubes and place in bacon drippings. Sauté until browned on all sides. Add tomatoes, red wine, beef broth, and cayenne to the pot, along with cooked bacon. Place onion, green pepper, and celery on top.

3. Lock cooker lid and bring to high pressure. Adjust heat to maintain pressure and process on HIGH for 25 minutes. Quick release pressure. Remove lid carefully to prevent scalding from escaping steam.

Spaghetti and Meatballs

What more can you say about spaghetti and meatballs?
Here is a quick and simple way to make this favorite.

2 tablespoons olive oil

I medium onion, chopped

3 cloves garlic, peeled and crushed

I 28-ounce can diced tomatoes

I 6-ounce can tomato paste

I cup red wine

I cup beef stock

I tablespoon dried basil

I tablespoon dried oregano

⅛ teaspoon red pepper flakes

Salt and pepper to taste

½ pound ground beef

½ pound ground pork

½ cup dried bread crumbs

¼ cup milk

I egg

I teaspoon salt

1. Heat oil in bottom of pressure cooker. Sauté onion until softened. Add garlic and continue to cook for another 60 seconds. Pour in tomatoes, tomato paste, wine, stock, and seasonings. Simmer gently to reduce and thicken sauce while preparing meatballs.

2. Combine ground meat with crumbs, milk, egg, and salt. Form mixture into twelve round meatballs. Pack them together firmly. Place meatballs in sauce, spacing them evenly.

3. Lock cooker lid and bring to high pressure. Adjust heat to maintain pressure and process on HIGH for 5 minutes. Quick release pressure. Remove lid carefully to prevent scalding from escaping steam. Adjust seasoning as desired.

4. Serve with cooked pasta and a garnish of grated Parmesan cheese.

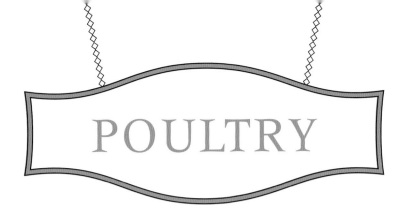

POULTRY

Barbecued Chicken Breasts

A finger-lickin'-good sauce on tender chicken breasts.

1 cup ketchup

¼ cup brown sugar

3 tablespoons Worcestershire sauce

2 tablespoons cider vinegar

1 dash hot pepper sauce

1½ teaspoons garlic powder

½ teaspoon dry mustard

½ teaspoon salt

3 tablespoons vegetable oil

2 pounds bone-in split chicken breasts, cut into halves

1. In a small bowl, mix together ketchup, brown sugar, Worcestershire, vinegar, hot sauce, and seasonings. Set aside.

2. Heat oil in pressure cooker. Add chicken pieces and sauté until browned. Pour sauce over chicken.

3. Lock cooker lid and bring to high pressure. Adjust heat to maintain pressure and process on HIGH for 10 minutes. Release pressure naturally. Remove lid carefully to prevent scalding from escaping steam.

4. Remove chicken pieces to platter and top with sauce.

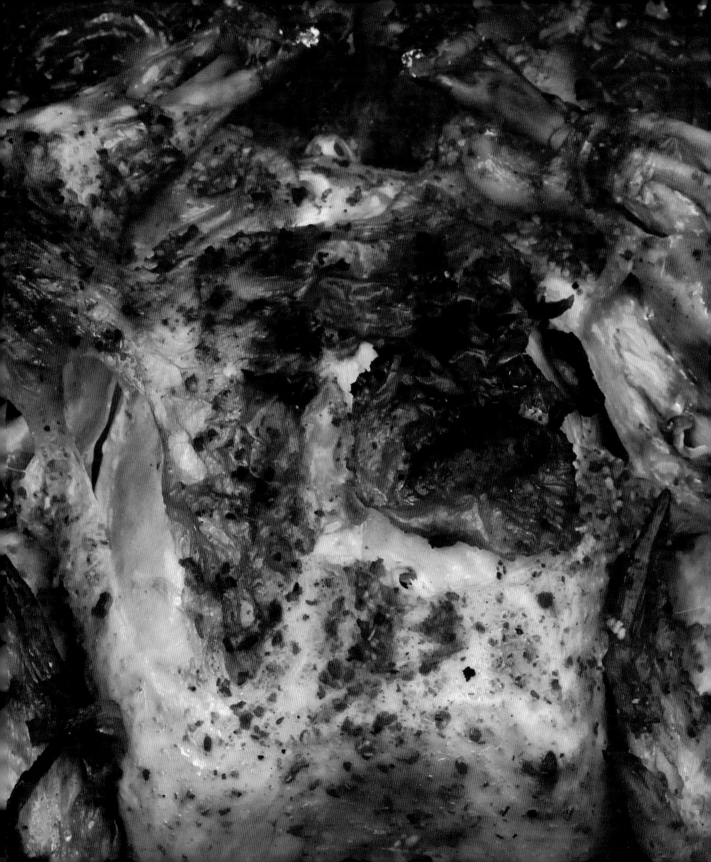

Cajun Chicken

A variation on Cajun sauce piquant, a family favorite.

2½–3-pound fryer chicken

½ cup flour

1 teaspoon salt

¼ teaspoon black pepper

3 tablespoons vegetable oil

2 cups sliced onions

1 green bell pepper, sliced

2 cloves garlic, minced

2 large tomatoes, chopped

1 8-ounce can tomato sauce

½ cup chicken stock

1 teaspoon Cajun seasoning (pg 97)

1. Cut chicken into pieces, and halve breasts. Coat chicken with flour that has been combined with salt and pepper.

2. Heat oil in pressure cooker. Add chicken and brown evenly on all sides. Add onions and pepper and continue to cook until softened. Add garlic, tomatoes, sauce, and stock, along with Cajun seasoning.

3. Lock cooker lid and bring to high pressure. Adjust heat to maintain pressure and process on HIGH for 10 minutes. Quick release pressure. Remove lid carefully to prevent scalding from escaping steam.

4. Serve with steamed white rice.

Chicken in Red Wine Sauce

A glass for you, a glass for the chicken. Now that's the way to cook.

2½–3-pound fryer chicken
½ cup flour
I teaspoon salt
¼ teaspoon black pepper
8 slices bacon
8 pearl onions, peeled
8 ounces mushrooms, sliced
4 carrots, cut into large chunks
I cup chicken stock
I cup dry red wine
I clove garlic, minced
½ teaspoon dried thyme
I bay leaf

1. Cut chicken into pieces, and halve breasts. Coat chicken with flour that has been combined with salt and pepper. Set aside.

2. In pressure cooker, fry bacon until crisp. Remove bacon and set aside.

3. Add chicken to the pot, and cook pieces in bacon drippings until golden brown on all sides. Stir in onions and mushrooms, and continue to cook for 5 minutes. (If there is excess fat, pour it out of pot at this time.) Add carrots and crumbled bacon, along with chicken stock, wine, garlic, and seasonings.

4. Lock cooker lid and bring to high pressure. Adjust heat to maintain pressure and process on HIGH for 10 minutes. Quick release pressure. Remove lid carefully to prevent scalding from escaping steam.

Cornish Game Hens

A sweet and tender dish. The wine enhances and balances the combined flavors.

2 tablespoons olive oil
2 Cornish hens, trussed
2 teaspoons paprika
I teaspoon salt
I teaspoon onion powder
I teaspoon dried thyme
½ teaspoon black pepper
I teaspoon cayenne pepper
¾ teaspoon garlic powder
½ cup dry white wine
½ cup chicken stock

1. Heat the olive oil and brown the Cornish hens on all sides. Combine spices and rub onto hens. Pour in wine and stock.

2. Lock cooker lid and bring to high pressure. Adjust heat to maintain pressure and process on HIGH for 10 minutes. Quick release pressure. Remove lid carefully to prevent scalding from escaping steam.

Forty-Clove Garlic Chicken

No, you're not trying to keep vampires away, though this might make for a good story over Halloween dinner. The garlic is surprisingly sweet and mild in this dish.

2 tablespoons olive oil

3 pounds of bone-in chicken breasts

Salt and pepper

2 fresh parsley sprigs

I fresh rosemary sprig

I fresh thyme sprig

I fresh sage sprig

40 peeled cloves garlic

I cup white wine

½ cup chick stock

I loaf crusty bread or baguette, sliced into rounds

1. Place oil in pressure cooker and turn to medium heat. Season chicken with salt and pepper and place in pot, cooking until browned on both sides.

2. Tie the fresh herbs together into a bouquet and add to the pot, along with the garlic cloves. Top with white wine and chicken stock.

3. Lock cooker lid and bring to high pressure. Adjust heat to maintain pressure and process on HIGH for 15 minutes. Quick release pressure. Remove lid carefully to prevent scalding from escaping steam.

4. Serve chicken with pan juices and spread garlic cloves onto rounds of fresh crusty bread.

Italian Chicken

*Pollo Italiano! No need to fry chicken cutlets to get the Parmesana flavor. Chicken simmered
in tomato sauce is all you need, especially if the sauce comes from garden tomatoes.*

2 tablespoons olive oil

2 pounds boneless, skinless
chicken breasts

1 medium onion, sliced

1 medium red bell pepper, sliced

6 cloves garlic, sliced

3 cups Italian red sauce,
homemade or jarred

½ cup red wine

1. Place oil in pressure cooker. Add chicken and brown on
   all sides. Top with onion, bell pepper, and garlic. Pour red
   sauce and wine over chicken.

2. Lock cooker lid and bring to high pressure. Adjust heat to
   maintain pressure and process on HIGH for 12 minutes.
   Quick release pressure. Remove lid carefully to prevent
   scalding from escaping steam.

3. Remove chicken and vegetables from pot. If the sauce is
   too thin, continue to cook until desired consistency. Serve
   chicken and sauce with cooked spaghetti and top with
   Parmesan cheese.

Peachy Chicken

Sweet and savory. You can also make it with fresh local peaches when they are in season.

3 tablespoons olive oil

1 pound boneless, skinless chicken breasts

1 tablespoon balsamic vinegar

2 cups chicken stock

1 15-ounce can peaches, undrained

1 tablespoon honey

1 tablespoon soy sauce

¼ cup cornstarch

¼ cup water

1. Place oil in pressure cooker. Add chicken and sauté to brown on all sides. Add vinegar and stock.

2. Lock cooker lid and bring to high pressure. Adjust heat to maintain pressure and process on HIGH for 10 minutes. Quick release pressure. Remove lid carefully to prevent scalding from escaping steam.

3. Remove chicken from pot and set aside. Add peaches, honey, and soy sauce to the sauce in the pot. Whisk together cornstarch and water and add to pot. Cook and stir until sauce thickens. Pour over chicken.

4. Serve with steamed rice and garnish with slivered almonds or serve over cooked noodles. Add freshly ground pepper to taste.

Jambalaya

My mother's jambalaya. She knew what she was doing.
Seriously. Get real andouillle if you can.

1 tablespoon olive oil

½ pound ham, diced

½ pound kielbasa or andouille sausage

1 pound boneless chicken breast, cut into small chunks

2 tablespoons Cajun seasoning (pg 97)

1 large onion, diced

1 green or red bell pepper, diced

2 stalks celery, diced

2 cloves garlic, minced

1 cup uncooked long-grain converted rice

1 cup diced tomatoes

½ cup tomato sauce

2½ cups chicken stock

1 pound peeled and deveined medium shrimp

1. Place oil in pressure cooker and set to medium heat. Add ham, sausage, and chicken to pot. Season with Cajun seasoning, and cook until chicken is cooked through. Remove meat with a slotted spoon and set aside.

2. To the pressure cooker, add onion, pepper, celery, and garlic. Cook until onions are translucent. Add rice, tomatoes, and stock.

3. Lock cooker lid and bring to high pressure. Adjust heat to maintain pressure and process on HIGH for 6 minutes. Quick release pressure. Remove lid carefully to prevent scalding from escaping steam.

4. Stir in cooked meat along with raw shrimp, simmering until shrimp are cooked through.

Cajun Seasoning

A staple in my kitchen. Perfect for blackened dishes and rubs.

2 teaspoons garlic powder
1 teaspoon onion powder
2½ teaspoons paprika
1¼ teaspoons dried oregano
1¼ teaspoons dried thyme
2 teaspoons salt
1 teaspoon ground black pepper
1 teaspoon cayenne pepper

1. Mix together seasonings and store in glass jar.

Old-fashioned Roasted Chicken

Honestly, there is hardly anything better than a simple roasted chicken.
Brown it well before putting it in the processor.

12-pound whole chicken

2 tablespoons vegetable oil

Salt and pepper

Homemade poultry seasoning (pg 100)

1 medium onion, quartered

2 stalks celery

2 cups chicken stock

2 tablespoons flour

1. Pat chicken with paper towels to dry. Rub oil over outside of chicken, and then season with salt, pepper, and poultry seasoning. Place onion and celery into cavity. Use string to truss legs together.

2. Heat oil in pressure cooker and place chicken into pot. Brown breast side first, and then turn until chicken is golden brown on all sides. Remove chicken from pot.

3. Add chicken stock to bottom of pot. Insert rack and place chicken on top. Lock cooker lid and bring to high pressure. Adjust heat to maintain pressure and process on HIGH for 15 minutes. Quick release pressure. Remove lid carefully to prevent scalding from escaping steam.

4. Lift chicken from pot and set aside on platter. Remove ¼ cup juice to a small bowl. Whisk in flour. Bring remaining juices to a boil. Whisk in flour mixture, cooking until gravy is thickened.

5. Season as desired with salt and pepper. Serve gravy with chicken.

Poultry Seasoning

It's very easy to make your own poultry seasoning to suit your taste.
And it's also so much cheaper to do so than to buy it in the store!

1 teaspoon ground sage
2 teaspoons paprika
1 teaspoon dried thyme
1 tablespoon salt
½ teaspoon black pepper
1 teaspoon garlic powder
1 teaspoon cayenne pepper

1. Blend together all ingredients.

2. Store in glass jar.

Weeknight Chicken Mediterranean

Fast and delicious, a favorite after-work meal.

2 tablespoons vegetable oil

2-pound boneless chicken breast, cut into 2-inch cubes

2 cloves garlic

2 tomatoes, seeded and chopped

½ cup sliced mushrooms

1 15-ounce can water-packed artichokes

½ cup Kalamata olives

¼ cup roasted red peppers

¼ teaspoon red pepper flakes

½ cup chicken stock

Cooked pasta

1. Place vegetable oil in pressure cooker. Add chicken and sauté quickly. Add rest of the ingredients.

2. Lock cooker lid and bring to high pressure. Adjust heat to maintain pressure and process on HIGH for 8 minutes. Quick release pressure. Remove lid carefully to prevent scalding from escaping steam.

3. Spoon chicken and vegetables over hot pasta. Sprinkle grated Parmesan, if preferred, and toss.

Simple Summertime Chicken Salad

I like to make big batches of chicken in the summer. This recipe is a favorite for turning leftover chicken into a quick afternoon lunch.

2 cups chopped cooked chicken

1 stalk celery, chopped

4 green onions, thinly sliced

1 carrot, shredded

½ cup red grapes, halved

1 tablespoon lemon juice

½ cup mayonnaise

½ cup slivered almonds

1. In a large bowl, mix together chicken, celery, green onions, carrot, and grapes. Squeeze lemon juice over mixture, and then fold in mayonnaise and almonds.

2. Serve as sandwiches or atop a green salad.

Sweet and Sour Chicken Thighs

The thighs are some of the tastiest parts of the bird. Thigh meat boasts
a great flavor that lingers on your tongue.

2 tablespoons vegetable oil

3 pounds bone-in chicken thighs

1 red bell pepper, cut into slices

1 medium onion, cut into half rings

2 carrots, peeled and cut into chunks

1 20-ounce can pineapple chunks

¼ cup brown sugar

½ cup vinegar

2 tablespoons soy sauce

1 tablespoon ketchup

½ teaspoon ground ginger

2 tablespoons cornstarch

2 tablespoons water

1. Heat oil in pot and brown thighs on all sides. Add red pepper, onion, and carrots. Drain pineapple juice from can and combine with water to make one cup. Stir juice together with brown sugar, vinegar, soy sauce, ketchup, and ginger. Pour over chicken.

2. Lock cooker lid and bring to high pressure. Adjust heat to maintain pressure and process on HIGH for 8 minutes. Quick release pressure. Remove lid carefully to prevent scalding from escaping steam.

3. Move chicken and vegetables to a serving dish. Mix cornstarch and cold water into a paste, and whisk into pot. Bring to a boil, and then reduce heat to simmer until sauce is thickened. Stir in pineapple chunks and heat through. Pour sauce over chicken.

4. Serve with rice.

SIDE DISHES

Baked Beans

Baked beans on a Saturday night were a tradition for us when we lived in New England. This recipe is delicious and it doesn't take all day.

I pound navy beans
½ pound bacon, diced
I medium onion, chopped
¼ cup brown sugar
¼ cup molasses
½ cup ketchup
I½ teaspoons salt
I tablespoon grainy mustard
½ teaspoon dry mustard
¼ teaspoon cayenne pepper
2 cups water (more if needed)

1. Rinse beans and soak in water at least 5 hours. Drain the beans, place in pot, and cover with fresh water. Bring to a boil for 5 minutes. Drain beans again and set aside. Preparing beans by this method reduces excess starch and helps beans retain their shape.

2. Sauté bacon until it starts to brown. Drain most of bacon fat off, leaving 1 tablespoon fat. Add onion, and sauté until softened.

3. Add beans. Whisk together brown sugar, molasses, ketchup, salt, mustards, and cayenne, and stir into beans. Pour in water, making sure beans are covered by 1 inch.

4. Lock cooker lid and bring to high pressure. Adjust heat to maintain pressure and process on HIGH for 45 minutes. Release pressure naturally. Remove lid carefully to prevent scalding from escaping steam.

5. Cook beans uncovered to reduce liquid, if desired.

Applesauce

Some people in my household can't eat a pork chop without a side of delicious applesauce.
We can hardly make enough to keep us through the winter!

6 Red Delicious apples, peeled, cored, and chopped

½ cup water

2 tablespoons lemon juice

3 tablespoons brown sugar

½ teaspoon cinnamon

¼ teaspoon nutmeg

1. Place all ingredients in pressure cooker. Lock cooker lid and bring to high pressure. Adjust heat to maintain pressure and process on HIGH for 3 minutes. Quick release pressure. Remove lid carefully to prevent scalding from escaping steam.

2. Puree sauce to desired consistency.

This recipe can be doubled. If you wish to can applesauce, process using a standard water bath per manufacturer's instructions.

Garden Fresh Ratatouille

In France it is called "ratatouille niçoise," in Greece "touriou touriou," and in Turkey "briam."
Here in the US, we just call it one of our favorite summer foods. But of course, it is good all year long.

1 medium onion, chopped

2 bell peppers, red, green, or yellow, seeded and chopped

3 tablespoons olive oil

2 cloves garlic, minced

1 medium zucchini, cut into half-moon chunks

2 large tomatoes, diced

1 large eggplant, peeled and cut into cubes

¼ cup water

½ teaspoon dried thyme

1 teaspoon salt

½ teaspoon black pepper

¼ cup fresh basil, cut into chiffonades

¼ cup fresh parsley

¼ teaspoon cayenne pepper

Salt and pepper to taste

1. Sauté onion and peppers in oil until softened. Add garlic and continue to cook for 60 seconds to release fragrance.

2. Stir in zucchini and tomatoes. Add eggplant, water, thyme, salt, and pepper.

3. Lock cooker lid and bring to high pressure. Adjust heat to maintain pressure and process on HIGH for 5 minutes. Quick release pressure. Remove lid carefully to prevent scalding from escaping steam.

4. Sauce should be chunky, and not watery. For a thicker sauce, remove a cup of vegetables and puree in food processor, and then stir back into sauce. Stir in fresh basil and parsley. Stir in cayenne pepper. Taste and adjust seasonings.

5. Serve hot, tossed with pasta or served over grilled chicken.

VARIATION

Add ½ cup Kalamata olives and serve at room temperature as a savory side dish.

Hoppin' John

This is a staple here in the mid-South. Smoked ham hocks and black-eyed peas were meant to be together—I would even say that they are soul mates.

6 cups water

2 cups dried black-eyed peas

2 large smoked ham hocks

1 medium onion, chopped

¼ teaspoon crushed red pepper

2 bay leaves

2 cloves garlic, crushed

1. Place water in pressure cooker. Add black-eyed peas that have been washed and drained to water. Place ham hocks, onion, red pepper, bay leaves, and garlic on top.

2. Lock cooker lid and bring to high pressure. Adjust heat to maintain pressure and process on HIGH for 10 minutes. Quick release pressure. Remove lid carefully to prevent scalding from escaping steam.

3. Remove ham hocks and let cool enough to handle. Remove meat from bones and mix into peas.

4. Serve over cooked white rice with your favorite hot pepper sauce on the side for added flavor.

Mushroom Risotto

An endlessly variable recipe—just change up the mushrooms and white wine,
and throw in some shellfish or chicken for a complete meal.

2 tablespoons olive oil

2 shallots, minced

8 ounces mushrooms, sliced thin

2 cloves garlic, minced

1 ½ cups arborio rice

½ cup white wine

4 cups chicken stock

4 tablespoons butter

⅓ cup freshly grated manchego cheese

Salt and pepper

1. Place olive oil in pot and sauté shallots and mushrooms until they are softened and golden, about 10 minutes. Add garlic and continue to cook for another minute.

2. Stir in rice and cook to toast grains lightly, about 3 minutes. Add white wine and cook another minute or so to burn off alcohol. Stir in chicken stock.

3. Lock cooker lid and bring to high pressure. Adjust heat to maintain pressure and process on HIGH for 6 minutes. Quick release pressure. Remove lid carefully to prevent scalding from escaping steam.

4. Continue to simmer over low heat, stirring constantly another 5–6 minutes, or until rice is tender. Stir in butter and cheese, and season with salt and pepper to taste. If needed, add a little more stock to bring to desired consistency.

5. Serve immediately, topped with Parmesan curls.

Risotto Cakes

Risotto can be mundane, but a batch of these little cakes, finished off on top of the stove and dressed with your favorite sauce, is another matter altogether!

3 cups leftover risotto
2 large eggs
½ cup fresh bread crumbs
¼ cup grated Parmesan
3 tablsepoons vegetable oil

1. Mix risotto, eggs, bread crumbs, and Parmesan. Form into balls and then flatten into patties. Dust lightly with additional bread crumbs.

2. Heat oil in a skillet over medium heat. Add patties and cook until they are browned on both sides.

3. Serve with your favorite sauce or a dollop of sour cream.

Spanish Rice

Color confetti rice with a hint of heat.

1 cup long grain white rice

2 tablespoons butter

1 medium onion, chopped

1 red bell pepper, seeded and diced

1 clove garlic, minced

2 cups chicken stock

1 large tomato, seeded and chopped

1 jalapeño, seeded and diced

2 teaspoons chili powder

1 teaspoon ground cumin

1. Rinse rice to remove starch and set aside to drain.

2. Place butter in pressure cooker and bring to medium heat. Add onions, bell pepper, and garlic, cooking until softened. Stir in rice to coat grains. Add chicken stock, tomato, jalapeño, and seasonings.

3. Lock cooker lid and bring to high pressure. Adjust heat to maintain pressure and process on HIGH for 3 minutes. Quick release pressure. Remove lid carefully to prevent scalding from escaping steam.

4. Fluff grains with fork and serve.

Perfect Long-Grain Rice Pilaf

Why buy a mix when the real thing is so easy to make?
For a side with beef, replace chicken stock with beef stock.

1 cup long-grain white rice
1 small onion, chopped
2 tablespoons olive oil
¼ teaspoon salt
¼ teaspoon ground allspice
¼ teaspoon turmeric
⅛ teaspoon curry powder
⅛ teaspoon black pepper
3½ cups chicken stock

1. Rinse rice to remove starch and set aside to drain.

2. Place oil in pressure cooker and bring to medium heat. Add onion and cook until softened. Stir in rice to coat grains. Add seasonings and chicken stock.

3. Lock cooker lid and bring to high pressure. Adjust heat to maintain pressure and process on HIGH for 3 minutes. Quick release pressure. Remove lid carefully to prevent scalding from escaping steam.

4. Fluff grains with fork. Remove from pot and garnish with slivered almonds, if preferred.

Savory Bread Pudding

Since when did bread pudding have to be sweet? This savory pudding, complete with lots of mushrooms and vegetables, is like your favorite holiday stuffing.

3 large eggs

1 cup milk

½ teaspoon Tabasco sauce

½ teaspoon salt

½ teaspoon black pepper

4 cups stale bread, cubed

1 tablespoon olive oil

1 medium onion, chopped

1 green bell pepper, chopped

2 cups chopped mushrooms

1 clove garlic, minced

2 cups chopped fresh spinach

1. In a bowl, whisk together milk, eggs, Tabasco sauce, salt, and pepper. Stir the bread cubes into the egg mixture and set aside.

2. Place oil in a large sauté pan. Add onion and bell pepper and stir until softened. Add mushrooms and garlic, stirring until moisture from mushrooms has evaporated. Stir in spinach, cooking until wilted.

3. Add the cooked vegetables to the bread and egg mixture, stirring until thoroughly blended. Place the mixture into a greased casserole dish. Cover dish tightly with foil.

4. Place 2 cups of water in pressure cooker. Place steamer basket into pot and set soufflé dish in basket. Lock cooker lid and bring to high pressure. Adjust heat to maintain pressure and process on HIGH for 25 minutes. Quick release pressure. Remove lid carefully to prevent scalding from escaping steam.

Soybean Salad

Think soybeans are boring? This salad combination makes soybeans the star.

1 ¼ cups dried beige soybeans

2 quarts water

1 teaspoon vegetable oil

1 tablespoon soy sauce

2 tablespoons rice vinegar

3 tablespoons vegetable oil

2 teaspoons mirin

½ teaspoon grated ginger

¼ cup chopped fresh parsley

2 scallions, greens and whites chopped

¼ cup dried cranberries

½ cup feta cheese

1. Rinse beans and soak in water at least 5 hours. Drain the beans, place in pot, and cover with fresh water. Bring to a boil for 5 minutes. Preparing beans by this method reduces excess starch and helps beans retain their shape.

2. Place soaked beans in pressure cooker with water and vegetable oil. Lock cooker lid and bring to high pressure. Adjust heat to maintain pressure and process on HIGH for 7 minutes. Release pressure naturally. Remove lid carefully to prevent scalding from escaping steam. Drain and set aside to cool.

3. Make dressing by combining soy sauce, vinegar, oil, mirin, and ginger in a shaker jar.

4. Stir chopped parsley, scallions, and dried cranberries into cooled beans. Stir in dressing and garnish with crumbled feta cheese.

Tex-Mex Pinto Beans

Once I started using the pressure cooker for beans, I have never made them
any other way. Spice your recipe up or down, as you prefer.

½ pound dried pinto beans

2 quarts water

¼ pound salt pork

1 tablespoon chili powder

½ teaspoon red pepper sauce

1. Rinse beans and soak in water at least 5 hours. Drain the beans, place in pot and cover with fresh water. Bring to a boil for 5 minutes. Drain beans again and set aside. Preparing beans by this method reduces excess starch and helps beans retain their shape.

2. Place beans in pressure cooker with water, salt pork, and seasonings. Lock cooker lid and bring to high pressure. Adjust heat to maintain pressure and process on HIGH for 5 minutes. Release pressure naturally. Remove lid carefully to prevent scalding from escaping steam.

VEGETABLES

Harvard Beets

What does Harvard University have to do with beets? Well, not much, really,
other than the fact that they share a similar coloring.

¾ cup white sugar
1 tablespoon cornstarch
½ cup white vinegar
⅓ cup water
1 pound beets
3 cups water
3 tablespoons butter
Salt and pepper

1. Place sugar, cornstarch, vinegar, and water in a saucepan on the stove. Stir ingredients together and bring to a boil, then simmer for about 5 minutes to thicken. Remove from heat and set aside.

2. Prepare beets by cutting off green tops. Leave the whole beet intact; do not trim ends. Wash thoroughly and place in pressure cooker with 3 cups water.

3. Lock cooker lid and bring to high pressure. Adjust heat to maintain pressure and process on HIGH for 20 minutes. Release pressure naturally. Remove lid carefully to prevent scalding from escaping steam.

4. Open processor and pour off cooking liquid. Place beets in colander and allow them to cool slightly. When they are cool enough to be handled, slip skins off under cold running water. Trim off ends and slice beets. Return to pot.

5. Add the sauce to the beets, and simmer for a few minutes to heat through. Before serving, stir in butter, and season as desired with salt and pepper.

Brandied Carrots

Though a fall favorite, these sweet brandied carrots are great all the time.

I pound baby carrots
¼ cup butter
¼ cup brandy
I teaspoon brown sugar
I teaspoon salt

1. Place carrots in pressure cooker in steamer basket with 2 cups water. Lock cooker lid and bring to high pressure. Adjust heat to maintain pressure and process on HIGH for 8 minutes. Release pressure naturally. Remove lid carefully to prevent scalding from escaping steam. Drain liquid from pot.

2. In a small saucepan, melt butter and whisk in brandy, sugar, and salt. Cook and stir until bubbly.

3. Stir sauce into carrots and simmer for 5 minutes until carrots are nicely glazed.

Mashed Cauliflower

Creamy mashed cauliflower is even better with cream cheese and garlic!

1 head cauliflower, cut into chunks
1 cup water
2 tablespoons cream cheese
2 tablespoons butter
3 mashed roasted garlic cloves
½ teaspoon salt

1. Place cauliflower in pressure cooker with water. Lock cooker lid and bring to high pressure. Adjust heat to maintain pressure and process on HIGH for 2 minutes. Quick release pressure. Remove lid carefully to prevent scalding from escaping steam.

2. Remove cauliflower from pot and drain. Add cream cheese, butter, garlic, and salt and mash together to desired consistency.

Whole Cauliflower with Cheese Sauce

A whole cauliflower drizzled in cheese is a great
centerpiece dish and always irresistible to the kids.

2 tablespoons butter

2 tablespoons flour

1 teaspoon dry mustard

¼ teaspoon salt

1 cup milk

1 cup shredded cheddar cheese

⅛ teaspoon cayenne pepper

1 whole cauliflower, core removed

1 cup water

1. First make cheese sauce: Melt butter over low heat. Blend in flour, salt, and mustard, stirring constantly until smooth and bubbly. Slowly add milk, stirring to incorporate. Continue cooking for 1 minute or until thickened. Stir in grated cheese and cayenne pepper, and continue to simmer until cheese is melted. Set aside.

2. Place whole cauliflower in pressure cooker with water. Lock cooker lid and bring to high pressure. Adjust heat to maintain pressure and process on HIGH for 5 minutes. Quick release pressure. Remove lid carefully to prevent scalding from escaping steam.

3. Place cauliflower on platter and pour cheese sauce over it. Sprinkle with paprika, if preferred.

Hot Pepper Vinegar

*Our kitchen wouldn't function without a jar of this on hand. It's good on
so many things. Try marinating chicken in it before grilling.*

Fresh jalapeño peppers
White vinegar

1. Wash peppers and slice them in half, removing the seeds. Finely dice them and pack into a jar.

2. Bring vinegar to a boil and pour over peppers, making sure peppers are completely covered. Add lid or cork to bottle and store in refrigerator for a couple of weeks before using.

Collard Greens with Brown Sugar

This is one of our son-in-law's recipes. If you aren't a big fan of collards, try this recipe—you will quickly change your mind.

2 cups ham stock (pg 40)

2 bunches collards, washed and sliced into 1-inch pieces

½ cup brown sugar

1 teaspoon salt

1 teaspoon pepper

1. Place the collard greens and ham stock in the pressure cooker.

2. Lock cooker lid and bring to high pressure. Adjust heat to maintain pressure and process on HIGH for 20 minutes. Quick release pressure. Remove lid carefully to prevent scalding from escaping steam.

3. Remove the collards to a serving bowl, and stir in sugar, salt, and pepper. Serve hot. Pass pepper vinegar at the table.

Corn on the Cob with Basil-Garlic Butter

Take this common summer food up a couple of notches with basil-garlic butter.

4 cloves garlic, peeled

20 leaves fresh basil

1 cup butter

Salt and pepper

2 cups water

4 ears corn, husks removed

1. Blend garlic cloves and basil in food processor until fine. Add the butter and a grind of salt and pepper, and process until smooth. Pack into bowl and refrigerate.

2. Place water in pressure cooker. Add steamer basket and place corn into basket. Lock cooker lid and bring to high pressure. Adjust heat to maintain pressure and process on HIGH for 2 minutes. Quick release pressure. Remove lid carefully to prevent scalding from escaping steam.

3. Remove corn and serve with chilled butter.

Lemon-Chive New Potatoes

An elegant side of potatoes in under 10 minutes.

12 new potatoes, halved
2 tablespoons butter, melted
½ teaspoon grated lemon peel
1 tablespoon lemon juice
2 tablespoons chives
½ teaspoon salt
⅛ teaspoon black pepper

1. Place one cup of water in pressure cooker. Arrange potatoes in steamer basket and insert into pot. Lock cooker lid and bring to high pressure. Adjust heat to maintain pressure and process on HIGH for 5 minutes. Quick release pressure. Remove lid carefully to prevent scalding from escaping steam.

2. In a separate bowl, whip together butter, lemon peel, juice, chives, and seasonings. Drain potatoes and place in bowl. Stir butter mixture into potatoes and serve.

Glazed Sweet Potatoes

Sweet and yummy. What more needs to be said?

6 medium sweet potatoes
3 tablespoons butter
½ cup packed brown sugar
3 tablespoons water
½ teaspoon salt

1. Peel and slice sweet potatoes into ½-inch chunks.

2. Place one cup of water in pressure cooker. Arrange potato slices in steamer basket and insert into pot. Lock cooker lid and bring to high pressure. Adjust heat to maintain pressure and process on HIGH for 5 minutes. Quick release pressure. Remove lid carefully to prevent scalding from escaping steam. Remove basket from pot and place potatoes in serving bowl.

3. Mix butter, brown sugar, water, and salt in small saucepan and cook over medium heat until sugar is melted and sauce is smooth. Pour over sweet potatoes and stir gently to coat.

Steamed Artichokes

One of our favorite meal starters. So elegant, and so simple.

6 artichokes

1 cup water

1 tablespoon lemon juice

½ cup mayonnaise

2 cooked garlic cloves, smashed

Salt and pepper

1. Prepare artichokes by slicing about ¾-inch off the top of the artichoke. If you push, use a kitchen scissors to trim off thorny tips. For large artichokes, slice the bottom stem off so the artichokes will sit comfortably in the basket. Smaller artichokes can be steamed with the stems. Just trim the end and peel the tough outer layer.

2. Place water and lemon juice in bottom of pressure cooker. Put steam basket with artichokes in place. Lock cooker lid and bring to high pressure. Adjust heat to maintain pressure and process on HIGH. Cook large artichokes for 15 minutes. Quick release pressure. Remove lid carefully to prevent scalding from escaping steam.

3. Blend mayonnaise and smashed garlic cloves, and season to taste with salt and pepper. Serve as a dipping sauce for artichoke leaves.

Sweet and Sour Red Cabbage

A great dish to complement some of our German meals.

1 medium head red cabbage
4 slices bacon, diced
1 small onion, sliced
¼ cup brown sugar
½ cup water
¼ cup apple cider vinegar
1 teaspoon salt
⅛ teaspoon black pepper

1. Shred cabbage, discarding core. Set aside. In pressure cooker, cook bacon and onion together until bacon is crispy and onion is cooked through. Add cabbage, brown sugar, water, vinegar, and seasonings.

2. Lock cooker lid and bring to high pressure. Adjust heat to maintain pressure and process on HIGH for 10 minutes. Quick release pressure. Remove lid carefully to prevent scalding from escaping steam. With the lid off, continue to simmer until desired consistency.

3. Add an additional tablespoon of vinegar if desired. Garnish with additional fried bacon.

DESSERTS

Rice Pudding

This desert was made just for the pressure cooker.
A comforting winter dish after a cold day of skiing.

1½ cups uncooked white rice
1 cup sugar
4 cups milk
1 tablespoon lemon juice
¼ teaspoon salt
1 tablespoon butter
½ cup dried cranberries
2 teaspoons almond extract
¼ cup slivered almonds

1. Mix together rice, sugar, milk, lemon juice, and salt in pressure cooker.

2. Lock cooker lid and bring to high pressure. Adjust heat to maintain pressure and process on LOW for 15 minutes. Release pressure naturally. Remove lid carefully to prevent scalding from escaping steam.

3. Stir in butter, dried cranberries, and almond extract. Garnish with slivered almonds.

Pineapple Bread Pudding

Kind of like a crazy, mixed-up upside-down cake!

4 eggs

1 cup sugar

½ teaspoon cinnamon

½ cup melted butter

1 15-ounce can crushed pineapple

2 cups bread cubes

¼ cup chopped pecans

1. Whisk eggs, sugar, and cinnamon together. Add melted butter and continue to stir until incorporated. Stir in pineapple and bread cubes. Pour into a buttered 1½-quart casserole dish and cover tightly with foil.

2. Put trivet in pressure cooker and place the casserole dish on top of it. Add two cups water. Lock cooker lid and bring to high pressure. Adjust heat to maintain pressure and process on HIGH for 18 minutes. Quick release pressure. Remove lid carefully to prevent scalding from escaping steam.

3. Remove dish from cooker and allow to rest 10 minutes before serving. Garnish with sweetened whipped cream.

Classic Cheesecake

Cheesecake in a pressure cooker? Yep. It's very easy and it saves a ton of time.
You can even make this after work for a fresh evening dessert.

1 tablespoon butter
½ cup graham cracker crumbs
19 ounces cream cheese
1 cup sugar
2 teaspoons lemon peel
½ teaspoon vanilla
3 eggs
1 cup sour cream

1. Butter a 7-inch springform pan. Sprinkle crumbs into bottom of pan and set aside.

2. In a large mixing bowl, beat cream cheese and sugar together until fluffy. Add lemon peel and vanilla. Continue beating, adding one egg at a time until mixture is smooth and light.

3. Spread mixture evenly over crumbs. Spray dull side of a piece of aluminum foil with cooking spray. Wrap pan tightly with oiled side down.

4. Place trivet in pressure cooker and add two cups water. Lock cooker lid and bring to high pressure. Adjust heat to maintain pressure and process on HIGH for 25 minutes. Release pressure naturally. Remove lid carefully to prevent scalding from escaping steam. Carefully remove baking dish and set on wire rack to cool.

5. When cool, loosen edge of cheesecake with knife before removing from pan. Top with thin layer of sour cream.

Index